Looking at

Animals in
the
OCEANS

Published by Raintree Steck-Vaughn Publishers,
an imprint of Steck-Vaughn Company

Series Editor Honor Head
Series Designer Hayley Cove
Picture Researcher Juliet Duff
Map Artwork Robin Carter / Wildlife Art Agency
Animal Symbols Arlene Adams

Raintree Steck-Vaughn Publishers Staff
Project Manager: Joyce Spicer
Editor: Pam Wells
Cover Design: Gino Coverty

Library of Congress Cataloging-in-Publication Data
Butterfield, Moira, 1961–
Animals in the oceans / Moira Butterfield.
p.   cm. — (Looking at —)
Includes index.
Summary: Provides an introduction to some of the different animals that live in the world's oceans, including the jellyfish, whale, manta ray, shark, starfish, sea cucumber, and others.
ISBN 0-7398-0107-4 (Hardcover)   ISBN 0-7398-0717-X (Softcover)
1. Marine animals — Juvenile literature.   [1. Marine animals.]
I. Title.   II. Series: Butterfield, Moira, 1961–   Looking at —
QL 122.2.B875   1999
591.77 — dc21   98-51599
CIP   AC

Printed in China
1 2 3 4 5 6 7 8 9 0 LB 02 01 00 99

Photographic credits
Frank Lane Picture Picture Agency: 12 J Nahmens/Earthviews; 14 K Aitken/ Panda; 15 Ian Cartwright; 27 D Fleetman/Silvestris. NHPA: 7 Daniel Heuclin; 26 Trevor McDonald. Oxford Scientific Films: 6 Max Gibbons; 8, 9 Richard Herrmann; 11 Peter Parks; 13 David Fleetham; 19, 22 Howard Hall; 20 Paul Kay; 21 Colin Milkins; 29 Kathie Atkinson. Planet Earth Pictures: 10, 28 Peter Scoones; 16 Marty Snyderman; 17 Pete Atkinson; 18, 23 Gary Bell; 24, 25 Doug Perrine.
Cover credit Sea cucumber: Planet Earth Pictures/Peter Scoones

Looking at

Animals in
the
OCEANS

Moira Butterfield

®
RSVP
**RAINTREE
STECK-VAUGHN**
P U B L I S H E R S
A Steck-Vaughn Company

Austin, Texas
www.steck-vaughn.com

Introduction

There are many oceans around the world. They stretch for thousands of miles. Some parts of the ocean are very deep and dark. Other parts are so shallow that you can see the bottom.

Hundreds of different animals live in the oceans, from brightly colored coral to dangerous sharks. Some live near the bottom of the ocean. Some live near the top. Some are the size of your hand, while others are the size of an airplane.

All these animals need to be able to swim and find food. Every animal has its own way of living in the ocean.

Contents

Sea Horse

A sea horse has a head that makes it look like a real horse. It has a long curly tail that it can wrap around seaweed. It has tiny see-through fins.

Its fins look as if they are made of tissue paper. The sea horse swims along by fanning them back and forth very fast.

Tuna

Tuna have shiny, silver scales all over their bodies. Their long, thin shape helps them to swim very fast through the water. They live in big groups called schools. Tuna is good to eat, so fishing boats hunt for the schools. The fishers try to catch as many tuna as they can.

Jellyfish

Jellyfish have see-through bodies that look as if they are made of jelly. They float around dangling their long, thin arms called tentacles.

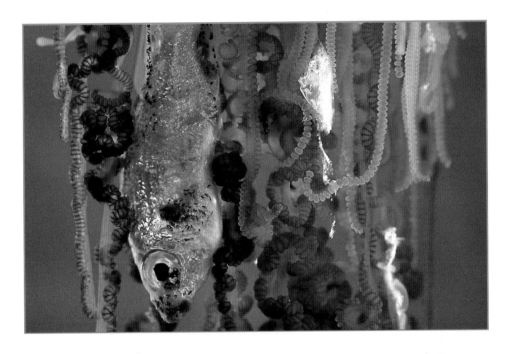

The tentacles have stingers on them that kill small animals. The jellyfish pushes the animal into its mouth to eat it.

Whale

Whales sometimes breach, which means they leap up out of the water. They are very long and heavy, so they make a big splash. When they are ready to dive, they flip their giant tails up into the air. Then, they swim down to the bottom of the ocean to find food.

Coral

Corals look like underwater rocks or plants, but they are really made of lots of tiny animals. They all live together in one place called a coral reef.

Some corals look like trees. Some are round-shaped like balls, and some spread out like pretty, feathery fans.

Manta Ray

A manta ray has a wide, flat body like a giant pancake. It swims by flapping up and down through the water, and it collects food at the same time. As the ray moves along, it keeps its mouth open. The ray catches tiny animals called plankton that float in the ocean.

Shark

Sharks have sharp teeth like rows of little pointed knives. There are lots of different kinds of sharks. The hammerhead shark is one of the fiercest in the ocean.

It has a big, wide head shaped like the end of a hammer. It uses it for bashing into other animals it wants to kill and eat.

Starfish

The starfish has lots of tiny tubes on each one of its arms. The tubes are its feet. It uses them to move along or to grip rocks. The starfish grabs animals in its arms and puts them into its mouth, which is underneath its body. If it loses an arm, it can grow a new one.

Octopus

An octopus has eight tentacles, with suckers all along them. It uses these tentacles to swim along. Then, it creeps up on other animals and jumps on them.

It wraps its tentacles around them and eats them. Some octopuses are brightly colored to show that they are poisonous.

Dolphin

Dolphins swim around in families. They are very clever, and they talk to each other with whistling and squeaking noises. They play together and help each other. If a dolphin is sick, other dolphins will help it to float along until it is better.

Butterfly Fish

Butterfly fish live around coral reefs. There are lots of different kinds. Some have a flat, round body like a plate. They are all brightly colored like butterflies.

If another fish like them swims by, they see that it is the same color as they are. Then they know it is a friend, not an enemy.

Sea Cucumber

A sea cucumber does not hunt other animals. It eats leftovers. It crawls along the seabed looking for tiny bits of food to collect on its sticky tentacles. Then it puts its tentacles into its mouth and sucks them. Sea cucumbers grow in lots of different shapes and colors.

Where They Live

This map of the world shows you where the animals live.

 sea horse

 tuna

 jellyfish

 whale

 coral

 manta ray

 shark

 hammerhead shark

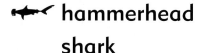 starfish

NORTH AMERICA

PACIFIC OCEAN

SOUTH AMERICA

 octopus

 dolphin

 butterfly fish

 sea cucumber

ARCTIC OCEAN

ASIA

EUROPE

PACIFIC
OCEAN

AFRICA

INDIAN
OCEAN

ATLANTIC
OCEAN

AUSTRALIA

Index of Words to Learn

coral reef A long line of coral rocks under
the sea. 15

fins Part of a fish's body, like a thin hand.
They help the fish to swim along. 7

plankton Tiny creatures that float in water.
Most are too small for us to see. 25, 27

scales Tiny, flat, but strong pieces or
plates. These thin plates overlap to
cover a fish's body. 9

school A big group of fish swimming together. . 9

suckers Round shapes on an animal's
body used to grip things. 23

tentacles Long, thin arms with no hands
or feet on the end. 23